OUR GIVING STORY

PUBLISHED by Mike LaBahn and Associates
BOOK DESIGN by Troy Hollinger

4616 Calavo Drive
La Mesa, CA 91941

mikelabahn.com

ISBN 978-0-9910043-5-5

TO MY

WIFE
CHILDREN
GRAND CHILDREN
GREAT GRAND CHILDREN
GREAT GREAT GRAND CHILDREN

Willie Sutton was an American bank robber – by profession – who managed to steal over $2 million during his 40-year criminal career. Once asked why he robbed banks, his wisdom was packaged in a simple answer: "Because that's where the money is."

Some people wonder why God talks so much about money in the Bible. The answer, offered by Jesus, is even more profound than Willie Sutton's: "Where your treasure is, your heart will be also..." (Matthew 6:21). God has always wanted your heart; the challenge is that it comes in the same package as your money.

Mike and Julie LaBahn have learned what God says about money from pastors and speakers, and their understanding of the Bible's teachings on the subject got them ready. The thing that elevated them into the extraordinary category: they took what they believed... and started living as if their beliefs were true.

I've watched them for over a decade, and their authenticity makes their message of biblical stewardship compelling. They're the real deal: take what God says about money, hear His promises about providing, understand His definition of stewardship, and then take actions that only make sense if He can be trusted. When that's your plan, faith is no longer an option: it is mission-critical.

How does someone aspire to return $1 million to the Giver when they're pushing their tired truck to get it started? What sense is it to go for the tithe – plus seven figures – when $100 for a new starter is beyond your reach? The story you're about to read is either a cute bedtime story, without a basis in fact, or it's the journal of a journey that you cannot explain apart from a God who says He is always ready and able to do immeasurably more than all we ask or imagine, according to his power that is at work within us.

Great stories take decades to live, weeks to record, but only hours to read. The potential of this story to change your eternity makes those hours a great investment in your never-ending future.

There's no ghost-writer embellishing Mike and Julie's account; you are sitting across the table from them at your favorite coffee house as you hear the story that comes from their heart, about the money that God put in their hands. Savor every sentence, and consider the story you're writing through your own stewardship!

FOREWORD / **BOB SHANK**

OUR GIVING STORY

SOME ASPIRE TO MAKE A MILLION.

WE ASPIRED TO GIVE A MILLION.

MIKELaBAHN

Standing there I could scarcely believe it. The pledge had seemed like it would be impossible to pay off, and yet it was paid. The years of strategizing, sacrificing, and working faithfully had ended in success, and our audacious goal was accomplished.

Our latest gift had completed our goal of giving away a million dollars over and above our tithes. Without context that may not seem so impressive – Bill Gates gives away millions every year, after all. But my wife and I are not Bill and Melinda Gates. We're ordinary people just like you, but we have one incredible advantage: we have understood and believed God's Word about finances, giving, and the blessings of generosity.

When I declared for the first time that my wife and I were going to give away a million dollars above our tithes, putting it into the Kingdom of God, people thought it was ridiculous. We were broke and broken, but God made a way. This is not the story of extraordinary talent or prodigious insight producing greatness; this is the story of two damaged people clinging fiercely to the Word of God, and as a result, churches were built, single mothers were taken care of, communities were given places to gather and grow, missionaries were sent out to the farthest corners of the world, and we found healing and comfort in our Heavenly Father's arms.

The following is our story.

Chapter 1

BROKE, BROKEN, AND BARELY SURVIVING

Because of our histories of lack, neither of us wanted to be simply Christians who tithed; we wanted to be givers.

When Julie and I were married on Saturday, August 12, 1978, gas was about 69 cents a gallon. As cheap as gas was then, it seemed to always be a struggle to keep it in our tank; our car learned to run on fumes. Furthermore, neither of us realized that our relationship with each other was void of the spiritual fuel we needed to make a marriage function. We soon discovered that we were running on fumes relationally, as well.

We both came from ragtag, fractured backgrounds. If you were to ask my wife if she has any fun memories from childhood you certainly won't get a quick answer, and you may not get an answer at all, despite her trying. She left home for the first time at 12, desperate to escape the dysfunctional and fatherless environment she had always known. By 16 she was living on her own. She managed to earn enough money to support her own apartment and purchase a car. The moment she graduated from high school she moved away. Too many bad memories in her hometown of Aptos, near

Santa Cruz. She wanted childhood to be over as soon as humanly possible.

I also came from a fatherless home and was kicked out of my house while still in high school, left to somehow make it on my own. No matter how strong a man is, there is no greater pain than hearing his own father say, "You are not my son. I am not your father." I was a boy when I heard it, and I was devastated. I had grown up in National City, but I was sent away to live in El Cajon. It was close enough to be frustrating, but too far to practically connect with all of my old friends in an age where 15 miles meant a long distance phone call and none of us owned a car. I might as well have been in Buenos Aires. Angry, confused, and friendless, I had to start over in a new town. I got out of the house I was sent to as soon as I could, but my life had changed by then. I hit the world with a chip on my shoulder, but I hit it alone.

You could say that we weren't exactly set up for success from early on in life.

When I was a boy of 12-years-old, something happened that I will never forget. I used to play games at the local boys' club since I didn't have anything else to do. I remember feeling so embarrassed because I did not even have 25 cents to buy a soda. Every kid, even the kids that were from single parent homes like my brothers and I, were given a quarter by their parents to make sure that they could stay cool and hydrated in the summer swelter. My brother and I had squat. I vowed to myself then and there that I would not raise a family in the way I had been raised; my kids would get a Coke whenever they pleased. While my peers were concerned about catching a baseball or kicking a football, my circumstances caused me to focus on my financial future. I determined I would do what others do to make a lot of money, and in my young mind that meant three options: build my own business, go into sales, or get a college degree.

Starting out, my wife and I both lacked the basic family life skills needed to make a successful marriage. There had been no emphasis on higher education or other things of consequence. We were birthed in dysfunctional families, raised in poverty, taught bad habits, and never given any instructions on how to handle money. Of course, we never had any extra money growing up. Still, no one taught us how to handle extra money if or when it did come our way.

HUMBLE BEGINNINGS

Looking back, even the beginning of our relationship was due to hard work and Providence. We met at the Hamburger House where I was working one of my two jobs in an effort to save money for my future. One evening while I was flipping burgers in my cook's hat and apron, Julie and a friend of hers walked in. We began to make eye contact through the restaurant, and Julie ended up returning several more evenings about the time

I was getting off of work. We eventually struck up a conversation and made plans to go on a date. As it turned out, I wasn't the only one working two jobs. Julie was also employed in two different areas, likewise trying to prepare for her future. Upon high school graduation, Julie had moved to San Diego. Her plan was to work and save money for nursing school. It was not easy for her to support herself as she had no family in the area to lean on.

Looking back on our early relationship, I believe we were both intrigued with one another in that we were one of those rare young couples that was determined to establish our own financial roots, despite having never been told to or taught how to do so. This common bond we shared attributed to a good part of the attraction we found for one another. Our dual desires to work hard and be prepared created many more meetings for us in the future.

On August 12, 1978 we married in a quaint, grassy park in Lakeside called Lindo Lake Park. We said our vows under a pepper tree in the hot San Diego sun, amid the geese and ducks that graced the small, quiet lake, with our closest friends and family there to share our union with us—well, most of them. Two of our relatives, one from each side of our family (both the opposite sex) were off smoking pot together during our vows. A touching show of familial support it was not. We exchanged wedding rings that we purchased at the Navy base for forty dollars each, and those same rings are still symbolizing those promises today. Our wedding reception, true to our financial capabilities, consisted of a potluck in the backyard of a friend's house – quite different than the elaborate weddings of today.

We were head over heels in love, and the future looked big and bright from where we stood. During our engagement, we had solidified plans to cofound a Mexican restaurant with my mother and stepfather in West Virginia. I had envisioned Julie and I opening our own restaurant one day, so this seemed like a great opportunity to gain some entrepreneurial experience. Her nursing school plans were placed on hold as we sold virtually all of our earthly possessions in order to make the journey. The day after our wedding we packed up the car and headed to West Virginia.

This move turned out to be a disaster on a number of fronts. First off, in West Virginia no one had ever even heard of a taco, let alone carne asada. Secondly, our plan was to live upstairs above the restaurant; the problem with this is my mother and stepfather lived up there as well. Obviously, living with your in-laws in a town of only 400 people is not the way to start a honeymoon or a marriage. After six weeks of tremendous tension, we decided it was best to return to San Diego. We sold just about everything to make the trip, and then we began the journey back to the West Coast. We were starting over, again, and once more it was with nothing.

Using my enviable math skills, I determined that the moths in our wallets wouldn't pay rent, and the only way we were going to make it until we got our feet under us was to find a way to live somewhere rent-free for a while. Finding a caretaking position was the only thing that leaped to mind, and so I searched the wanted ads in the newspaper every day for six months as we struggled to get by, each of us working two jobs. In all of those six months, I came across zero ads of the type we were looking for, until one day there were two right there in front of me: "Caretaker Wanted." One was in Jamul, the other in El Cajon.

Julie and I got in the car. As we drove, I told her I wasn't going to leave until we had the El Cajon job. We got the job that day. It was a one-acre estate where we could stay in a guest house and be caretakers of the property in exchange for free rent. This was on top of each working two jobs already, and now Julie had to tend to the needs of an elderly woman, and I had to tend the entirety of the grounds! As crazy as it was, this arrangement allowed Julie to finish her courses and earn an LVN (Licensed Vocational Nurse) certification at a community college.

THE RELATIONSHIP VOID

When we married, we were young people (early twenties) with relationship voids the size of moon craters. We did our best with what we knew at the time, worked a variety of odd jobs, and attempted to establish our life together. Julie once described the early years of our marriage as a bad toothache. You can feel there is a problem, yet you delay fixing it, hoping it will get better on its own. Unfortunately, any time you put pressure on it, it gets inevitably worse. We began to have all the tell-tale difficulties of a troubled relationship: lack of communication, lack of relating physically on an intimate level, and disputes and differences of just about every kind. Difficulties and conflicts plagued our marriage, yet we strove to smooth out the obvious fractures.

In hindsight, it wasn't long before we discovered (though we weren't aware of it at the time of our engagement) that the things we did not have in common greatly outweighed the things we did have in common. Seemingly, the only real commonality we shared at that point was a desire to create a better life for ourselves.

Early on in our marriage we became Christians. Julie began attending church with some friends of ours, and I would join them later in the morning for breakfast. After Julie accepted the Lord, she began to turn her attention to my salvation as well. She and her friends decided to change the breakfast rules; they said if I wanted to go to breakfast, I had to go to church. That didn't seem like such a bad deal, and less than a year later, I was saved as well. We don't always come across as the most emotional people in the world, and maybe we aren't, but Julie must have cried every single Sunday that first year. It was abundantly clear to both of us that God was working on our hearts in a very real way. We realized how much we had to be thankful for, and we committed to following Jesus for our entire lives.

This happened fairly early on in our marriage (thank the Lord), and we began to submit ourselves to the process of centering our lives and marriage on God's principles through studying His Word.

A PLAID COUCH AND A BEAST

While our marriage started to improve, our finances seemed destined to remain in the unpleasant category of "barely surviving." After returning to San Diego, Julie and I both worked at two full-time jobs for two years. Our entrepreneurial spirit unbroken, we did this in order to save enough money to help support ourselves as we began our own business. We had no business experience, little education, marginal skills, and very meager capital. What we did have was a willingness to work hard, a desire to be self-employed, and a sincere earnestness to help others. Yet while the business was getting off the ground, certain material sacrifices had to be made. Enter the plaid couch and the beast.

We owned a nightmare of a plaid couch that desperately needed to be replaced. The seats on the couch were permanently attached to the frame and could not be removed. As the fabric became worn, the springs in the seats started to pop up and jab people when they sat down. We couldn't blame the manufacturer; it was a cheap, three piece set which we purchased for $250. Even back then that was a bargain!

Eventually, the pillows flattened out, the stitching broke, the plaid pattern faded, and the couch started to unravel. We dutifully covered the seats with blankets so guests could sit down without getting skewered. It was horribly uncomfortable to sit on, and it was embarrassing to invite others to do so. When we had people over for gatherings, it was awkward for both them and for us. Three times we tried to save up the money to purchase a new couch, and each time our fledgling business had a financial need that became the top priority. We felt defeated.

The feeling of defeat not only came in plaid, but also in two-tone beige and yellow. Our tan-paneled station wagon, the kind you hear people vow they'll never drive when they get old, was aptly named The Brown Beast. Because of an engine badly in need of repair, the wagon could be heard clanking its way down the street just before sending up smoke signals into the sky. It would occasionally lock us in or out due to a short in the electrical system. By this time we also had children in tow, which made this situation even more problematic and extremely inconvenient.

One summer, on a much-needed, long-overdue family vacation to a quiet and quaint town nestled in the San Jacinto Mountains of Southern California, we had just begun to enjoy the tall pines, sweet-smelling cedar, rock formations, and hiking trails. This "escape" turned into a major vexation when the motor mounts snapped and the engine fell out on the road. To make matters worse, while the car was being repaired, the entire family came down with food poisoning! (I've been suspicious of diner ketchup ever since.)

Something had to be done to get our life and our finances under control. We were walking with God, attending church, and doing what we needed to do to survive. At some point in our early family life, the pastor of our church, Robin Hadfield, said something that changed our lives forever. He said, "If God can go through you with money, He will." We began to learn about biblical, financial principles, and then we learned about tithing. This concept of giving God ten percent of our income immediately became a part of submitting ourselves to God. The prophet Malachi spoke clearly to us:

Bring the whole tithe into the storehouse, so that there may be food in My house, and test Me now in this,' says the Lord of hosts, 'if I will not open for you the windows of heaven, and pour out for you a blessing until it overflows. Malachi 3:10

Though our business accountant advised us that we could not spare the ten percent, we continued to tithe. We wanted to do everything God said to do, even if it was a leap of faith every time we offered it to Him. We believed the words of Jesus when He said, *It is more blessed to give than to receive.* (Acts 20:35)

Because of our histories of lack, neither of us wanted to be simply Christians who tithed; we wanted to be givers. We determined to be givers who gave more than our regular tithe, regardless of how little money we were making.

This commitment seemed risky, considering how tight our finances were at the time. We were barely getting by, but we knew there was always someone who had it worse than us, and it became our desire to help those in need with whatever resources we had. We started buying gasoline on a regular basis for five single moms from our church, but that about drained our financial resources. We knew that despite a lack of funds, we could do more. If we could not give dollars and cents, we gave minutes and hours. Single moms in our church were desperate for any kind of assistance. Our hearts were set on serving, so we gave what we had. We gave our time to transporting and cheering on their children at sporting events, helping with car and home repairs, and providing childcare.

We later learned that we were practicing a biblical principle which we will discuss in detail in the next chapter. Looking back, we see how our hearts were purified in the process, as we learned to give in so many different ways. Every time we gave, it required sacrifice and was often inconvenient. God was teaching us faithfulness with what He gave us.

He who is faithful in a very little thing is faithful also in much. Luke 16:10

Chapter 2

SMALL STEPS, BIG CHALLENGES

As our business grew, we mistakenly believed our financial situation would quickly improve.

We started LaBahn's Landscaping in 1981 with a rather limited vision to mow lawns for money. Our business plan was essentially the more lawns we mow, the more income we can generate. We continued to work full-time jobs while launching our new business. Because neither of us knew much about how to handle or budget money, we always seemed to be under immense financial pressure. Our lack of financial understanding impacted both our business and our personal finances.

Our company truck was a Datsun 1600 flatbed, 4-speed stick shift, painted green with spray paint. We called it the "Green Beast" because, like the station wagon, it could be heard roaring down the road long before it could be seen. We would routinely push the Beast, popping the clutch just to get the stubborn monster started so we could go from one job to another. We performed this ritual with the Green Beast countless times because we could not secure enough money in our business bank account to even replace the starter.

One of the jobs we performed besides mowing lawns was to create fire prevention "safe zones" for clients by clearing their lots of brush and weeds. I tried to do the majority of the heavy work, but there were times when Julie had to drive the Beast to the dump and single-handedly unload heavy branches and brush despite her petite, 5-foot, 95-pound build.

As our business grew, we mistakenly believed our financial situation would quickly improve. However, as our growth increased, so too did our accounts payable and accounts recievable. It became obvious that we were going to have to make some adjustments in our financial structure. We had fallen significantly behind with all of our suppliers and constantly struggled to meet payroll.

We were embedded in debt. So many of our checks bounced that the bank threatened to close our account. Soon enough we realized that if our bank wouldn't accept us as customers, neither would other banks. When the next check bounced, the bank called and informed us that we had until 1:00 PM that day to bring in enough money to cover that check. On the verge of losing our bank account (and essentially our business), I acted fast. I could only think of one thing to do. I hopped in my car and went looking for the mailman. He usually delivered the mail at 4:00 PM, but that would be much too late to meet the bank's demand. Knowing I had a check due to arrive that day, I found our mailman who took the same route every day and never seemed to be in much of a hurry. I explained to him my urgent situation and pleaded with him to let me get into the vehicle in order to find the check. Although at first not willing to break post office policy, he eventually dug through the van and found the check himself. Making it to the bank just in time, we had once again narrowly escaped disaster.

In another desperate situation, I again drove forty-five minutes each way to collect a check that was overdue. Again I made it to the bank in time and insisted the teller hand-post the check since we were overdrawn once again.

Minutes after I arrived home the bank called and told me the IRS had just levied my bank accounts, including the check just delivered and hand-posted. We knew we owed the IRS money; we had even made arrangements to make payments with the IRS and had agreed to a specific day that the total amount would be paid off. However, during that time, people often made arrangements with the IRS to make payments but they didn't always follow through. So even though we had an agreement with them that they should have honored, they chose to levy our accounts, both personal and business. Of course, this same day we were scheduled to pay our employees. With no other option than the notorious "quick loan," we agreed to pay exorbitant interest charges, only increasing our debt.

Nothing seems as scary in hindsight, but having all of our funds levied by the IRS and going into even deeper debt to pay my employees made me angry.

Julie was scared; I was sick and tired. At one point, brooding on the impossibility of it all, I had to pull the car over to vomit. I wasn't ill, just experiencing such intense strain that my body responded physically. It was a terrifying and frustrating time financially.

OUR EARLY GIVING JOURNEY

It was in the midst of this incredible financial stress that I came up with a financial goal that has paved the way for our giving journey. Sitting in a taco shop, eating carne asada and rolled tacos, and trying to figure out what we were going to do with the chaos of our finances, I took a paper napkin and wrote: We are going to give away one million dollars – above our tithe – into the Kingdom of God.

Naturally, that statement seemed absurd. Julie could only ask, "How the heck are we going to do that? We can't even afford to buy a starter for our truck!" Though impractical for a young married couple with more expenses than profits, this vision set us in motion to get out of debt and bring order to our finances. It was a goal God placed in our hearts, and we were inspired by it. He spoke hope into our hopeless situation.

I began listening to motivational tapes by Zig Ziglar, John Maxwell, and other great leaders. I was allowing my mind to be reshaped by speakers who understood that ordinary people can do extraordinary things. My spirit was being refreshed and counseled by Bible passages that spoke to me in a new way. For the first time, I began to believe that man was designed by God to achieve great, meaningful things.

MINISTERING TO SINGLE MOMS

God first tested our willingness to be faithful to Him in the smaller areas of our lives. We began to help others and give in small ways. As we did, God increased our capacity to give. We began to realize that opportunities were everywhere and all it took to see them was the heart to look. Single moms came into our lives and we took pleasure in filling their gas tanks, providing lunch money for their kids, and taking their children to their soccer games. We counseled them, watched and even helped discipline their kids, cooked dinner and did chores for them, anything that could make their lives a little easier. They valued our time as much as they appreciated the financial help. We were learning what it meant to "stand in the gap" for others on both practical and spiritual levels.

I searched for a man among them who should build up the wall and stand in the gap before Me for the land. Ezekiel 22:30

We were so broke that we could not even afford that stupid starter for our truck. We had no real plan to accomplish our goal set that night in the taco shop. But we had a heart for the forgotten, the suffering, and in particular (due to our

backgrounds), for single moms. We prayed that we
could live out Paul's teaching:

*At this present time your abundance being a supply
for their need, that their abundance also may
become a supply for your need, that there may be
equality.* 2 Corinthians 8:14

The Bible is far from silent on this issue, as you
can see. It is our responsibility to care for the poor
– even if we are poor ourselves! Generosity is not
limited to the wealthy or the prosperous. There are
people in need all around us.

I always think back to an interview I once read
between former President Jimmy Carter and CNN's
Carol Costello from October 11th, 2002. Jimmy
Carter was receiving the Nobel Peace Prize that year
for his work through the Carter Foundation. Costello
asked him about his worldwide charitable activities,
and he told her that it was a priority to reach the
unreached and the needy. "These are the poorest and
most destitute and forgotten people in the world,
and that's where the Carter center does its work."

It's my opinion that we ought to do the same. James
1:27 tells us:

*Pure and undefiled religion in the sight of our God
and Father is this: to visit orphans and widows in
their distress, and to keep oneself unstained from
the world.*

No matter how bad off we were, we weren't orphans and we weren't widows, and some people out there were. The Bible's mandates were clear to us. We couldn't put off giving, and yet even as we gave we wanted to give more, though oftentimes it didn't make sense financially.

Somehow we would continue to be givers. Towards that end, we learned all we could about money. It was clear to us again that getting out of debt was our first priority.

Chapter 3

CRAWLING AND CLAWING OUT OF DEBT

...you can accomplish things bigger than you can ever imagine if you follow God's biblical principles.

I took responsibility for this learning curve. I read everything I could get my hands on, starting with Larry Burkett's *Money Matters: Total Financial Control God's Way*. I knew I didn't have the answers or the practical experience to solve the debt problem facing us, but the Bible did. Christian authors such as Ron Blue and Dave Ramsey shaped my understanding of biblical stewardship.

The more Julie and I discussed and digested the material, the deeper our commitment grew to run our business without any debt whatsoever. The story of the plaid couch was just one of many examples where we determined to honor our commitment to live debt-free. Even in those early years it was counter-cultural to avoid the trap of easy credit, practice financial discipline, and pay cash for a new couch. We even replaced that ugly, two-toned, self-locking station wagon only after we had saved enough money to pay cash for a used van. The lessons we had learned about credit and debt guided us through the decades. For over 20 years, we did not purchase anything for the business on credit. Having gone through the heartache and heartbreak, not to mention the blood, sweat, and tears of paying off debt, we became debtaphobics. When we needed new equipment, new trucks, or new computers for the business, no matter what the expense was, even though credit was readily available to us, we would simply wait until we had the money to purchase what was needed. We were getting better and better about the principle of not going into debt. We were now experiencing a new kind of freedom. We were free to give into the Kingdom of God, not tied up in the chains of creditors.

COLOR-CODED DEBT DESTRUCTION

I made a color-coded chart listing every vendor to whom we owed money. We voluntarily put LaBahn's Landscaping on a cash basis with our suppliers and made a schedule with them to methodically pay down our debt. Many companies were willing to let us pay down our debt and pay cash for new supplies. If ever we could not afford the monthly payment we had agreed to make, I would initiate a phone call at the earliest possible moment and discuss the matter, usually paying something in good faith. They were always surprised when they received a phone call like this. I was informed that people usually avoided their creditors when they weren't going to be able to make an entire payment, but that didn't sound honest to us. I could hear the voice of an old preacher saying, "If you can't pay something, say something."

Each vendor had its own color: Hydroscape was blue, Ewing Irrigation was pink, and so on. As a visual person, I had to see the progress on the chart, with what we owed at the top and columns with spaces for each month's payment. Any unbudgeted income went to pay down a debt.

As one example, we landed a job in La Jolla, a wealthy beach community of San Diego. We were to put in sod and a large sprinkler system. Because of the scope of the project, we profited a nice sum. The amount we profited was exactly the amount we owed Hydroscape, so we paid off a large debt to them entirely, not even buying so much as a Slurpee out of that check.

God knows what we are going to do before we do it. We believe that is why He gives us extra money, and, likely, why other times He doesn't. If we have learned the lesson He is trying to teach us, He will come into our situation, often in a way that is totally unexpected.

THE LANDSCAPE STARTS TO CHANGE

If our company were to significantly grow, it became apparent to us that we would need to begin transitioning from residential to commercial properties. We would need to move from mowing lawns to maintaining building complexes.

One day while out canvassing for jobs, I met a fellow who told me that the president of his HOA was his landlord. Phone number in hand, I quickly followed up on the lead which led to this HOA president giving LaBahn's Landscaping a try. (This same president/landlord became my longest-lasting and dearest friend.)

The condo complex sat on 22 acres; it was so large that one could not see from one end of the property to the other. Honestly, we were unsure how we would ever handle this account which was well beyond the single family homes we normally serviced. I didn't sleep well for days. Deep inside, though, I knew it was an opportunity I couldn't turn down. God had developed my personality in such a way that I had become comfortable with being uncomfortable. I knew I could trust Him.

Commissioned to keep complete care of this condominium complex, we mowed lawns, repaired irrigation systems, and did everything else the property required. It did not take long before we realized how little we actually knew about landscaping on a large scale. I enrolled in the local community college and took courses to broaden my knowledge base.

After learning a great deal in school and even more the old-fashioned way, we were confident we could take on more condominium contracts. Primarily due to our sophisticated marketing program of knocking on office doors and trying to find a point of contact, we were able to secure more contracts relatively quickly. We bought equipment, hired a couple of employees, and I continued to take classes related to landscaping.

The next step became clear: my writing skills had to improve if I was to continue to do bids and other reports. I wandered up to the general education building on campus and ended up signing up for a writing class. Eventually I realized that if I kept at it, I would end up with a college degree. This feat required rising at 3:30 AM most mornings to study, exercise, and head for work by 6:00 AM. Because I was in my late twenties and early thirties, I had the energy to pursue this goal despite the many demands on my time. After I worked all day, I loaded up Julie and the kids and drove wherever needed to deliver bids, stopping for dinner on the way home. After 13 years of this and basically one class per semester, I graduated with a bachelor's degree.

EYE-PATCH SALESMAN

It was during this time of commercial growth in LaBahn's Landscaping that a seemingly unfavorable situation turned into an incredible opportunity. While on a job site in Santee, I was in the process of adjusting a sprinkler head that was tucked underneath a shelf next to a building and behind a bush. I attempted to adjust the sprinkler head without turning the water off and gave it just a little twist. In an instant, the velocity of the water pressure caused the sprinkler head to shoot off furiously. Of course there was no time to move, and my eye took the impact full force. The doctor told me that incident was the equivalent of getting hit in the eye by Muhammad Ali. I had a serious injury and was diagnosed with a detached retina.

Bedridden in the hospital for two weeks and bored out of my mind, I had plenty of time to think about business strategies. It was during this time I came up with a novel idea. Wearing an eye patch and a less-than-discreet hospital gown, I snuck out of my hospital room in search of the supervisor or executive in charge of landscaping the hospital grounds. I am sure I looked ridiculous, but, nevertheless, I introduced myself and asked if he would accept a proposal for the landscaping of the hospital and its affiliated locations.

At the time, Kaiser Permanente was under contract with another landscaper, but the supervisor asked me to call him in six months when the contract was up. I took out my calendar and said, "Morning or afternoon?" He said it was my choice and I told him I would call him June 1 at 9:00 am. He smiled at me, standing in my open-backed nightgown, and I'm sure he thought, "Sure you will." Well, June 1 at 9:00 AM I dialed his number, and lo and behold he said, "I've been expecting your call."

He ended up hiring us for a very small office building, but a couple of years after that the entire San Diego region of Kaiser came up for bid and he called me and asked us to bid the whole region. By God's perfect timing and grace, we landed a huge client.

During the contract negotiations, I asked

the purchasing agent if there was some way we could shorten time period in which they would pay us for services rendered. Naturally, the agent became nervous, as though she'd discovered a red flag with our company. She communicated to me their expectation that their vendors be financially solvent. She must have noticed my apprehension and consequently asked for the Dunn and Bradstreet report for LaBahn's Landscaping. "You do have one, right?" she inquired.

"Of course I do!" I replied, feigning certainty.

"Could you please have it on my desk by tomorrow morning?" the agent asked.

I had NO idea what a Dunn and Bradstreet report was, so I immediately called my accountant who explained. "Mike, a D and B report describes the health of your company in four main areas: financial data, trade payments, company size, and years in business."

"Okay, well, I need one. Tomorrow," I responded ignorantly.

"Mike, these reports take ten days to turn around. There's no shortcut to this process." His news was staggering. I was forced to call the purchasing agent and tell her the bad news. I knew the great opportunity I had been chasing since my three-years-ago-eye-patch-pitch was about to end.

To my surprise, the agent's secretary answered the phone and relayed that a family emergency was expected to keep the purchasing agent away from the office for... ten days. Upon her return, the Dunn and Bradstreet report was on her desk and negotiations resumed. Even more miraculous was that she suggested we get paid quarterly and in advance!

We could hardly believe what was happening to us. Up to this point we had grown accustomed to driving all over town, picking up checks from people who owed us money just to pay our bills and avoid bounced checks. Before the contract even began, we drove together up to the hospital headquarters and collected a six-figure check for work yet to be performed!

What a process of transformation! The blessing of God became more and more tangible as we faithfully committed our profits to Him. The pattern we were following was to be willing to be uncomfortable and to think bigger than we would normally think. We understood that He knew what we would do before we did it, and we began to recognize His moves on our behalf. We have a strong conviction that the hospital contract happened because of our goal to give away a million dollars to the Kingdom of God.

We learned something else very significant during this period. There are always going to be naysayers. You know, those people who, no matter how big or small your dream, feel it's their job to tell you it can't be done. One New Year's Eve, Julie and I were out to dinner with a couple who were friends of ours. During the conversation, I predicted that one day our business would gross a hundred thousand dollars a year. Everybody at the table laughed, yet currently, we are on our way to $15 million a year. Another night I predicted that someday the company would have five trucks on the road, and I would get personalized license plates, LaBahn 1,2,3,4, and 5. Again people told me this would never happen, but currently we have 60 company vehicles on the road. In my early days I said I would like to become a motivational speaker.

Again, people told me that would never happen, but God's grace is greater than the doubters. I now speak nationally and internationally. A few years back I was the keynote speaker at a pastors' conference in Cuba; four years before that I was speaking at a conference in Cambodia. From time to time Julie and I are travel around the country telling our story to raise money for the Kingdom of God.

I firmly believe God takes the ordinary people of the world and does extraordinary acts through them, but those ordinary people must be willing to attempt to accomplish things they know they cannot do without God's help. We can accomplish things bigger than we can ever imagine if we follow God's biblical principles. Those acts of obedience plant the seeds to release God's favor and harvest into our lives.

Chapter 4

STEP-BY-STEP GIVING

We usually never knew where the funds would come from, just that we wanted to give and would do whatever it took to honor our pledge to God.

It is our conviction that a giving ministry doesn't happen all at once by writing a huge check. We feel strongly that if a person has not been giving regular offerings unto the Lord when they have little money, they are not likely to start giving a large amount if they come into money through an inheritance or some other form of windfall.

From our experience in the ministry of giving, what defines a giver is not what amount is given but the amount of sacrifice. When it was a sacrifice to give a bag of groceries to a single mom with kids, we gave. We believe it was and is a supernatural process. Now our sacrifice is much larger, and the joy of honoring the Lord with our finances runs deep. We simply can't outgive God.

SUPPORT THE LOCAL CHURCH FIRST

When the concept of the million dollar pledge to God first came to us in the taco shop, we did not have clear direction of where to give. We were already in the habit of giving to worthy ministries as we had the opportunity. What we weren't sure about was, beyond our tithe to our local church, where to give larger offerings. After consulting with respected pastors, we settled on giving the majority of our gifts to the various ministries of our own local fellowship. As long as the church is not stagnant, we believe the wise giver should plant his offerings based on what God is doing in their local church, as the income of the local church is limited to only those who attend there.

INTENSIFIED GIVING STARTS IN OREGON

At one point in our marriage we decided to move the family to Oregon and build a home there. I was able to operate our business in San Diego long distance by fax and email, and we were excited about a new community for our family. We were a part of a thriving, growing church in Eugene, Oregon. Not long after we joined the Eugene Christian Fellowship, our pastor, Gary Clark, called for a special offering for a worthwhile purpose. He stressed it was time for an offering of significant sacrifice, a "first fruits offering," above our tithe.

Honor the LORD from your wealth and from the first of all your produce; so your barns will be filled with plenty and your vats will overflow with new wine. Proverbs 3:9-10

We were being asked to make a significant sacrifice at a very inopportune time. We were already trying to fund the building of our home in Oregon, and it wasn't exactly going along smoothly due to the Oregon rains and other costly delays. Yet, the Lord confirmed for us that it was His timing, no matter our concerns. Julie and I were in agreement, up to a point. I felt the pledge, because the construction on our home was not complete, should total $25,000. Julie, who has always demonstrated more faith than I in these matters, was pushing for $50,000. It was an amount I had a hard time swallowing, being that unexpected costs routinely arise in building projects. What if we had to stop construction on our home? What an inconvenient time to give so much! Especially when we were finally in a position to do something big for ourselves!

Finally, the decision was made, and the $50,000 was pledged. It was inconvenient, because we knew it could stop the progress on our home. It was sacrificial, more than we had ever given before. Yet we longed for God to deepen our faith and knew that this was the step we were to take.

About a year later, relieved that our home was more or less finished and our pledge was paid, our church was challenged once again by our pastor to fund a very important project. Knowing that what was finally settling back to normal would be upended again, we dug deep and gave sacrificially again, this time doubling the amount.

This church in Eugene, Oregon, had a strong emphasis on world missions: equipping, supporting, and sending out missionaries to share the Gospel of Jesus Christ and to love the communities into which they were sent. We gave these two "first fruits" donations to the general fund, but we were well-aware that the church was very good about managing money. No televangelist was buying a private jet with our money. People desperate for the Gospel received missionaries, in part because of the gift God used us to give.

Once we started giving, it did not stop. The following year, we changed churches in order to attend worship services and participate in the ministries of a church closer to our home in Cottage Grove, Oregon. Riverside Community Church of God, led by Pastor Rick Haberly, had a terrific heart for discipleship, and they were about to start building a family center. We decided to give 10% of the overall cost of that center, regardless of how big the final sum became. The idea was to provide a place for conferences, potlucks, sports teams, and community events, all for the purpose of getting unsaved individuals "in the parking lot." Once in the church's realm of influence they would have access to programs to help them through hard times, introduce them to people dedicated to serving and loving selflessly, and most importantly, they would be given opportunities to hear the Gospel. Through our gift and the generous gifts of others, the idea became reality. Even though we were in a much better place financially than when we first started, the Lord was stretching us with our giving. Each gift still required a tremendous amount of faith.

SAN DIEGO COMPLICATIONS AND CHALLENGES

We lived in Oregon for a total of 10 years, and as time progressed, we found we missed San Diego and our friendships there. Unfortunately, in 2004 the housing market was peaking and it was a difficult time for buyers. We sold a newer house in Oregon only to pay twice the amount for an older home in San Diego. To make matters worse, the real estate market crashed soon after and the value of our purchase in San Diego dropped dramatically.

Untimely as it was, our new church in San Diego, Foothills Christian Church, was in the midst of a building campaign to construct a larger sanctuary. We attended a campaign dinner with the congregation to learn more details about the expansion program, and we were challenged to make a three-year pledge, not of equal giving, but equal sacrifice.

Foothills was, and still is, a trustworthy and influential institution in the surrounding community. One of its main goals is to reach the next generation for Christ, which they do by ministering to thousands of young people each week. Through their Youth Venture Teen Centers, church volunteers meet at-risk youth and provide them with the sort of stable, loving environment that Julie and I never had – and they take them to church if they want to go, too. A dedication to obeying God's Word and following His principles had grown the church drastically, and they were running out of space. They had been good stewards, and we knew that we had to help out.

The theme of equal sacrifice had already taken root in our hearts, as we had been learning this on our journey of faith in giving. All givers are equally valuable and treasured in the eyes of God. The biblical concept is best illustrated by the story of Jesus observing the poor widow at the temple.

And He sat down opposite the treasury, and began observing how the people were putting money into the treasury; and many rich people were putting in large sums. A poor widow came and put in two small copper coins, which amount to a cent. Calling His disciples to Him, He said to them, "Truly I say to you, this poor widow put in more than all the contributors to the treasury; for they all put in out of their surplus, but she, out of her poverty, put in all she owned, all she had to live on." Mark 12:41-44

In light of our circumstances due to the housing market, I tried to apply common sense to the situation with a pledge I thought would be sacrificial. But Julie said she felt God was telling her to give something much more substantial. Knowing that God was calling us to give sacrificially, we pledged $100,000, a large sum but less than the previous campaigns in Oregon. While we had three years to pay off the pledge, finances became uncertain when complications arose in our business. LaBahn's Landscaping was facing management problems and experiencing dwindling profits. We truly had no idea where the money to fulfill that pledge was going to come from, yet we trusted God to provide what we felt He had asked of us to give.

Looking back on those first pledges, we had to see and accept that faith was required in each circumstance, regardless of the financial situation we were facing each time. We usually never knew where the funds would come from, just that we wanted to give and would do whatever it took to honor our pledge to God. We reflected on Solomon's words:

He who watches the wind will not sow and he who looks at the clouds will not reap. Ecclesiastes 11:4

Just after we began to make payments on our three-year pledge, southern California, quite literally, caught fire. San Diego had suffered a severe drought, and the east county mountains and fields were teeming with dry brush. One of our larger clients recognized their exposure to fires, and they hired us to remove the extensive brush surrounding all of their properties. On this one extra job we made close to $50,000. Shortly after that brush-clearing job was completed, one of our client's landscaping caught on fire. That particular job paid $50,000. When that check came in, it went straight to pay off our pledge to the church building campaign. We had completed a 3 year pledge of $100,000 in 6 months! God has a way of coming through when we have the faith to trust Him. It is well to mention that we normally only made a couple thousand dollars on any extra job. Julie and I cannot possibly view these two extra jobs as a coincidence.

After the completion of the three-year period, Foothills Christian Church held another fundraiser, yet this pledge was supposed to span a period of only one year. Common sense kicked in again, and I thought to myself, if I did a three-year pledge for a hundred thousand dollars, then mathematically a one year pledge should be a sacrifice of about $30,000. Once again, the Holy Spirit prompted Julie to challenge me on that. She said that amount was absolutely ridiculous. Well the wheels were turning in my head, and I believed I had a way of outsmarting her (and God), while still pledging a sacrificial amount. Since Foothills had just concluded their three year pledge one year earlier, I figured the church wouldn't be able to raise very much money this time around. So I told Julie that we would pledge 10% of the total amount of pledges the church raised in one year. Good old common sense told me they'd raise about $300,000, bringing our pledge to the $30,000 I'd originally wanted to give. I'd be able to manage that.

Much to my surprise, the church was able to raise 1.6 million dollars! I knew it would take me several years (well past the one year deadline) to pay off our 10% pledge. In my attempt to outsmart my wife (and God), I inadvertently pledged $160,000. At one point during this very humbling payment process, I met with one of the staff pastors and told him I didn't think I'd be able to honor my pledge. He wisely told me not to tell him but to tell God. Five years later we paid off our pledge of $160,000.

A PROVEN, FINANCIAL, SPIRITUAL PRINCIPLE

Once we formed a mindset to become givers into God's Kingdom, the financial resources for that pledge always opened up! **The more we gave, the more God blessed us.** In the process, our faith increased, and as you will see in the final chapter, our vision expanded.

Chapter 5

ORDINARY PEOPLE, EXTRAORDINARY GOD

God puts a vision into the hearts of men. Men then decide how to respond to that vision.

There have been many bumps on the rocky road of our giving journey, only a few of which we have shared in this short book. The entire time we have traveled on this adventure, God has always been faithful to pave His way over those pesky bumps. We have experienced serious seasons of financial drought where we could not imagine a scenario where God could come through, but we always trusted that somehow, someway He would. At times we wondered if we would ever achieve the seemingly impossible financial goal put on my heart to plant one million dollars into the Kingdom of God.

On the day we finally decided to add up our giving to see how close we were to fulfilling our pledge, we were wonderfully surprised to find out we had not only met but exceeded the goal. We hadn't even been tracking it, just loving the giving, and in doing so, had unwittingly met our goal.

Literally, in spite of ourselves, and even with some very poor financial decisions and blunders early on in the business, God proved faithful to us time and time again, honoring our hearts and our intentions to bless His Kingdom.

Know therefore that the LORD your God, He is God, the faithful God, who keeps His covenant and His lovingkindness to a thousandth generation with those who love Him and keep His commandments. Deuteronomy 7:9

Remember, God's financial plan for your life will not always add up and make accounting sense on paper, but it will always work. He always comes through with the provision you will need to fulfill His plan for His purposes.

DON'T LOOK AT CIRCUMSTANCES

We determined to give away money during all seasons, even during the recession of 2008, regardless of how much or how little income was coming into our business at the time.

Sow your seed in the morning and do not be idle in the evening, for you do not know whether morning or evening sowing will succeed, or whether both of them alike will be good. Ecclesiastes 11:6

As we gave, God steadily provided. At a time when there was very little building and new construction taking place in our area, God provided a very profitable installation job. Soon after, a gas tanker truck tipped over on one of our client's locations. Their predicament ultimately turned into our provision. We took the enormous job with gladness and continued to give of our profits.

It's a simple spiritual reality that we see over and over. God can take anyone and do great things with his or her life! Just look at Peter and John; they were unschooled, ordinary men who demonstrated great courage because they had personally been with Jesus.

Now as they observed the confidence of Peter and John and understood that they were uneducated and untrained men, they were amazed, and began to recognize them as having been with Jesus.
Acts 4:13

God does not require any spectacular giftedness or extreme talents. If He did, He would have looked right past us and moved on to another couple far more qualified to fulfill His plan. What we love about this is that we are just like Peter and John, the epitome of normal, ordinary people, lacking the experience and formal education for the job at hand; and yet, He chose to use us because of our availability, not our ability.

GOD GIVES VISION

God puts a vision into the hearts of men. Men then decide how to respond to that vision. Those who possess a desire to cooperate with Him will start to obey the challenge, counting on God to supply the provision. You've read our story, one of broken beginnings, limited means, progressing to achieve a goal of giving a million dollars. What can He do with you?

THE PATTERN OF INSANITY

Some would say we were insane to even attempt to give a million dollars into the Kingdom. We rather like that label. Our co-senior pastor of Foothills Christian Church in El Cajon, David Hoffman, loves to relate the famous quote, "Insanity is doing the same thing over and over again and expecting a different result." For us, in God's spiritual world, "insanity" means doing something that is seemingly irrational or, in man's eyes, impossible, to further the work of the Gospel.

When we were sitting in that taco shop so many years ago, dreaming of a flourishing business and God-sized gifts, there was no rational line of reasoning that indicated that we could ever give away a million dollars. It was an "insane" idea given to us by the all-powerful, all-knowing God. On paper, we were the wrong people for God to choose to work through. In truth, I didn't receive a clear mandate from God, a supernatural vision, or a deep voice roaring out of the heavens. There weren't instructions each step of the way down the path of our giving. He never sent an angel or a brilliant light to strengthen us and exhort us with a resounding, "Fear not!" We never felt a special anointing. None of that happened.

Instead, we were and we remain just two God-fearing, God-loving people who read His Word and apply it to the fire of daily living. In that process, we learned some pretty valuable lessons on how God can use us if we just open up our hearts and our pocketbooks for His work. He shows us the need; we take that as our call to action.

EXTRAORDINARY NEW GOALS

Already our giving has opened the doors to building churches, sending out missionaries, reaching out to needy communities, and equipping ministers with the tools needed to carry out their vision. What could happen with ten times that amount of money? A hundred times? Our faith and follow-through are the only limiting factors.

Chapter 6

THE GIVING PLEDGE

What would happen in your financial life over the next 30 years if you set a goal to give away a certain amount of money?

Understand that God has instilled unique abilities in each of us for His glory, not ours. He has gifted some with the power to make wealth beyond what their family needs.

But you shall remember the Lord your God, for it is He who is giving you power to make wealth, that He may confirm His covenant which He swore to your fathers, as it is this day. Deuteronomy 8:18

The question now is: How are you going to use your God-given abilities to acquire wealth so that He can further his Kingdom through you? We have shared our story openly and transparently because our hope is that it will challenge and inspire others to give into the Kingdom of God. Perhaps you own your own business, or maybe you are in the early part of your working years. We want to encourage you to set a goal for giving that far exceeds what you could do on your own. Have you ever tried to do something that is beyond yourself and requires

God to achieve it through you? When was the last time you trusted God and did something for the first time? In reality, most of the things we attempt to do are those things we know we can do.

It was the pastor/author/speaker John Maxwell who first planted the seed in my life to dare to seek God for something beyond myself, for something great. When God gave me the challenge to give away one million dollars in that taco shop, it seemed to lie dormant for many years. Yet, all the while, a nurturing of the gift of giving was in progress. We partnered with God over a very long time to see this come to fruition.

What would happen in your financial life over the next 30 years if you set a goal to give away a certain amount of money? How would God move in your life? We hope you will set a giving goal that makes absolutely no sense in the natural with the abilities you currently have. It should be a goal that makes you cry out, "Oh, Lord!" It should bring you to your knees, which is a blessed place to be.

Would you prayerfully consider partnering with us to generate $100 million for the work of the Gospel? Would you be willing to give Him what could only be obtained with Him, just like us? If you are led to participate in our giving ministry, would you go to MikeLaBahn.com and let us know? (We will NOT solicit you for donations, but we will suggest books or other resources for your growth and encouragement.) We simply want to record these giving pledges as a collective record to gain a sense of how the Holy Spirit is touching hearts all around the globe to stand with us for the Kingdom of God. Please go to our website and tell us: "God has put on my heart to give $_____ over the next _____ years into the Kingdom of God."

Let's be clear: God is looking for sacrifice from all of us. For some that will be a million dollars or more. For many that will be significantly less. After the tithe, commit to give until you start to have to cling to the Father for help. Even as you read this, Julie and I are embarking on a new, personal pledge. We are trusting God to help us give away much more plus inspire others to give the ten million dollars during our remaining years.

We serve a God of limitless resources. Our prayers, requests, and thoughts are often too small, and our expectations are too low. What an opportunity to demonstrate a holy boldness! Will you dare, along with us, to attempt great things for God and expect great things from God? This is a distinguishing mark of not only the New Testament era church, but of many churches around the world even now. I love an Oswald Chambers quote that I refer to often: "If you believe in Jesus, you are not to spend all of your time in the calm waters just inside the harbor, full of joy, but always tied to the dock." What does he mean by this? He wants you to be unhindered, sailing the waters of freedom, blessing, and giving with abundant generosity.

We know that we will be blessed for taking God's Word seriously and living a life of generous giving, but what else could happen?

Missionaries could reach all corners of the globe, disabled children could receive the help that they need, wells could be dug, Bibles distributed, churches, schools, and hospitals could be built. Communities could be transformed, disciples could be made, the poor taken care of, and Christ's light could be shown to a greater extent on the earth. Faith and generous giving empower these visions. Where God is leading you, be sure to follow. It can be nothing less than extraordinary.

Thank you for praying and seeking God in joining this lawn-mowing couple's "grassroots" effort to gather ordinary people who dare to do extraordinary things!

Epilogue

GOODBYE FOR NOW

What's the first thing you think when you sit down to hear a sermon and discover it's going to be about money? What about when a friend recommends that you read a book on giving? If you're anything like most people, your first response might be to feel a little apprehensive or overwhelmed. Some people even feel resentful, as if they already know they'll be conned or forced to do something against their will.

If one's arm needs twisting in order to get them to give, that is a sign of spiritual sickness. Although they may not be used to the idea in the beginning, spiritually healthy people want to give. Because they are so thankful for what their Father in heaven has freely given them, it is hard to stop growing Christians from giving!

Have you heard (or made) these excuses for not giving generously?

"I've worked hard for my money; after my tithe and taxes, the rest is mine!"

"I give to charities in my community; why should I also give to the church?"

"I simply can't afford it!"

These excuses lose their weight when compared with Scripture. The Psalmist declares,

The earth is the LORD'S, and all it contains, the

world, and those who dwell in it. Psalm 24:1

For every beast of the forest is Mine, the cattle on a thousand hills...And everything that moves in the field is Mine. Psalm 50:10-11

Sometimes we need a reminder that the principles outlined in the Bible for Christian giving are not for God's benefit but for ours.

Other books by Mike LaBahn:

Giving God's Way
Radical Generosity Will Change Your Life

Proverb's Practical Principles
Universal Truths from the Book of Proverbs

Get Free
*A Short Guide to Financial Well-Being from The
Wisdom of Proverbs*

Available at **mikelabahn.com**